Contextuality

A Value Generation Framework

for

Business and Society

Pieter Marais

First published in 2009 through CreateSpace

Printed and bound in the USA by CreateSpace

About the author

Pieter Marais has a Masters Degree in Psychology and is a registered psychologist with the Health Professions Council of South Africa. He completed various business development and consulting training programmes and courses internationally, including programmes at leading South African and UK universities.

He worked in consulting capacity, as business owner and for consulting firms, also in employment capacity for various companies, in the Organization Strategy, Design and Development domain. In his career he consulted to companies in various industries e.g., resources, finance, media, medical, retail, manufacturing, services, government, research and utilities. He consulted in various countries including the USA, UK, Canada, Australia, Peru, Brazil, Chile and various countries in Africa – South Africa, Zimbabwe, Swaziland, Namibia, Botswana and Ghana. He was part of the original team that introduced Levels of Work (SST) into South Africa that formed a cornerstone philosophy in consulting work in different parts of the world. He trained numerous people, as principle trainer, on the framework and technologies, in most of the regions mentioned above. He was co-founder and director of BIOSS South Africa.

Business and organizational **contexts**, the understanding thereof, the implications and the practical application to organizations and people remains key in his approach. Defining the nature of, setting up for and dealing with **context** (an expert domain), as manifested in e.g. Stratified Systems Theory, is an area he considers critical to successful organizations. He has been and still is actively involved in advancing research and technology development, as well as facilitating development, in this domain, to continue shaping the knowledge and application depth. Some of this research, as applied to companies and people, will be captured in follow-on books. He has an equally passionate interest in Scenario Planning and futures research as he considers this to fit in with the contextual suite of technologies and processes that appropriately contextualise, focus and gear successful companies for the future.

This book is dedicated to:

1. My many colleagues over the years for:
   - their challenges that assisted in pushing the boundaries for further development,
   - their learning they have been so keen to share,
   - their willingness to learn and experiment with new developments.

2. My wife, Christella, who has been and continues to be my best colleague, sharpest challenger, creative contributor and most patient supporter.

3. My children, Caro and Ruan, for their constant push to see the product in print.

Index

Preface

The series of books, of which this is the first, have been long in the making. It captures years of collegial and personal contextual experience, action research, understanding and collegial in-depth knowledge development. This was undertaken and gained through work within and consulting to companies. Thousands of individual work-based interviews across the full spectrum of the organizational hierarchy, executive to labourer, as well as individual work and contextual capability interviews have contributed hugely to this pool of knowledge.

While Elliot Jaques provided us with the breakthrough broad principles, the in-depth translation of context, complexity and complex systems into and within organizations, uncontaminated by e.g. grading systems, has not been done or written down adequately for public access. Various individuals, consultancies and organizations have utilised the broad principles reasonably effectively. There is however a contingent amongst these entities, that has unfortunately contaminated and compromised the true value to the detriment of organizations as well as individuals. There are current versions where a little SST (Stratified Systems Theory) knowledge and a large component of grading knowledge have led to the "gradification" of SST. This contamination has contributed to confusion and the de-valuing of the huge potential value-add of this framework to organizations. This and other issues convinced me to embark on writing this series of books.

As a group of colleagues we have deliberately, over a period of 20 years, continued to develop a deep level understanding of the principles and intent behind SST and how this translates and manifest in the work environment. It was done through active involvement in a wide variety of companies from multiple industry sectors, having conducted thousands of work context, content and capability interviews (originally using the CPA process developed by Gillian Stamp and over the past 7 years using the WCI, a process developed by myself). This plus educating a vertical cross-section of people in organizations on the framework in various parts of the world (developed and emerging economies) have lead us to the point where we have significantly enriched the knowledge and understanding of the generic themes, the clusters of work, as well as its content. It has advanced the understanding of the work done by Jaques and others, and also contributed to a better clarity of concepts.

Through the years and through the introduction of terminology in an attempt to better explain the subtleties within the frameworks, confusion often resulted. This came about as a result of attaching "activity" words rather than contextual descriptors to a particular level. These activity words became commonly used language across the organizational spectrum, but often used in a way that resulted in an inappropriate interpretation of the level of work complexity and context. Referring for example to level 3 as the level of Best Practice has become a misnomer. Best Practice has become a generic term, like strategy, and does not necessarily reflect the contextual level and its value contribution. Gillian Stamp, through her organization mapping process, tried to explain how these translates at different levels - that quality, service and best practice can be found at all levels. Unfortunately, individuals in organizations often tend to get "stuck on words". The moment the phrase "best practice" comes up people immediately equate this to level 3 – which more often than not, may be completely wrong.

Using fractals to explain specific organizational actions and how this translates into different emphases at different levels may be a more appropriate way to convey the information. Fractals imply that at all levels all themes will be present but in a more or less complex format. For example the themes of finance, innovation, knowledge work, people, quality, practice, service, parallel process, strategy, etc. will be present at all levels but the underlying complexities, drivers, the dynamics as well as actual value contribution and its value delivery will be different. The challenge is to identify and define the appropriate fractal presence of these themes as they present within each contextual level of work. The appropriate identification and definition thereof will assist in realising the appropriate pitch of contribution at the appropriate contextual level. This will be expanded on in the second book dealing with Context and the Organization.

The more advanced and in-depth understanding of the context of work at each level, as a result of research, development and practice, has culminated in a better appreciation of:

- How work fits together into a coherent whole;
- How these wholes group into sensible clusters (contexts) of VALUE ADD to an organization;

- What the actual "theme content" of each cluster or context of work really is about. This should not be confused with the content level of education or remuneration that needs to be attached to an individual role. In company practices, for example grading systems, a number which dates from the 1960's linear and predictable economies, combined with a resultant inappropriate focus on qualifications, often created confusion regarding the aspects of context and content. This confusion has done organizations and individuals a disservice and sometimes actively destroyed value as it resulted in unrealistic expectations and subsequent inappropriate actions. The difference between context and content will be further explored in this book.
- How these themes translate into appropriate:
  - Organization scenario and strategy development;
  - Organization design and setup, including appropriate systems;
  - Measurement of deliverables;
  - People appropriateness in terms of contextual capability and development.

These are some of the aspects based on a contextual framework that has moved beyond theory. It has become a well researched scientific basis for dealing with context, organizations and people. This has opened the exciting prospect of scientifically designing VALUE GENERATING (as in deliverables) organizations, moving past the notions of hierarchy of authority, importance, size of reward, years of experience, inappropriate lists of qualifications, size of organization and number of subordinates, etc. VALUE ADD, the context thereof, the dynamics and processes within and the resultant delivery are the key aspects of this framework. In many organizations where a contaminated version of the framework was introduced, a process of unlearning will unfortunately have to take place, if they claim to be SST or contextually based. The original value generating qualities of the framework were often destroyed as a result of contamination through superficial knowledge. Some organizations and individuals have for example been "sold up" on their "higher level pitch" and "higher level of capability". This resulted in the continuing, but absurd, notion that higher is necessarily better.

An understanding of the real contexts of value-add will demonstrate that:

1. Higher is not necessarily better, it can sometimes be inappropriate;
2. Lower is not necessarily lesser but can in effect sometimes be more desirable;
3. Vertical is not necessarily advancement, in fact, horizontal is often hugely more advantageous;
4. Lower is not reserved for the illiterate, highly skilled professionals are also present here;
5. Higher is not reserved for people with an endless paper trail of qualifications, in fact, the paper trail in certain instances are just that, a paper trail. Higher level value add often manifest without formal qualifications as it originates from a deep level understanding and dealing with context;

6. Remuneration is not (should never be) a vertical debate, even more so since the world started challenging the value of vertical hierarchies of status. The value of contribution by experts at "lower levels" has become high in demand, especially in a knowledge based economy. The continued focus on vertical hierarchies does not cater for appropriate remuneration and reward strategies in a different world of work. Vertical hierarchies as such, as well as the practice of vertical hierarchical parallel pay bands for line management and specialists, are under pressure in the current world of work, but will get onto even more "shaky ground" in the emerging future world of work.

At this stage I do not want to explore the above statements any further. These, its emergent global basis, its current format as well as implications for organizations will become clearer, not only from the content of this book, but also from others to follow.

I trust this first book will evoke enough debate and assist existing users, that may have been put on the "wrong pathway", to revisit and "put things right" and to extract the huge value embedded in the framework. New users may use this to start challenging their existing paradigms.

I trust there will be a renewed and growing appreciation, amongst all, of the timeless contextual value of the framework. Within this timeless contextual framework, continuous solutions for the now and the future can be developed or contextualised for value contribution. The **contexts** of this contextual framework seem to have enduring and globally transportable timeless value, providing the framework within which appropriate design and development takes place. The **content, within each context** may therefore have to adapt continuously to suite the emerging world. The framework will however provide a continuous and stable framework for describing context.

It will take courage to move into this new brave world with its contextual challenges and exciting opportunities, or (re)discovery and continuous learning of the new things that, in many instances, still need to be developed. The scientific basis, timeless nature and global transportability of the framework and its ability to define contexts, will go far in assisting us to deal with the challenges of this new world we live in.

Pieter Marais   *e-mail: maraisp1@iafrica.com*
                                        Mobile: +27 82 8298188

Contextuality

Introduction

Significant changes have taken place in the global domain of business over the past 50 years - the two main shifts were:

- The shift from the "Simple Linear" to the short interval of perceived Chaos - shift one;
- Shift two – from the short interval of perceived chaos to the current and still emerging quantum and complexity framework.

This can also be seen as a shift from a pre-modern and modern "dogmatic" and predictable era to a post-modern "diverse" era with less rigid and less predictable agendas.

In the world we live in today there is a presence of both, old and new, (pre)modern and post-modern. Sometimes these diametrically oppose one another often resulting in conflict. The old dogma wants to enforce a "right way of looking at the world" while the younger era people see the world more flexible, relative, diverse and more inclusive. Younger employees manage to accommodate dogmatic opinion as just another opinion about the world and do not allow these opinions to hold them hostage. If flexibility is not on the agenda, they search for better opportunities as the world increasingly allows for flexibility and scope, as a result of globalisation, to "go somewhere else". The old dogmatism in companies often contributes to employee turnover especially in companies where historical practices are still maintained at all cost in this world of diversity and change we live in today.

Let us try and understand the nature of the shift, which is still in process and will continue to impact the way we see and treat the world around us, a bit better.

The Contextual Shift

Key Points:

1. *Within the ongoing volatility and change around us, there are patterns of consistency that are clearly identifiable and globally transportable.*
2. *The same generic patterns, or themes, are identifiable and present globally – from sophisticated to non-sophisticated environments.*
3. *Contextuality explains the nature of and value adding concepts attached to each contextual theme or level.*
4. *Understanding and managing context will increasingly become a key differentiator between more successful and less successful companies.*

Changes taking place in the world today emulates what complexity scientists have been busy with for a number of decades. The nature of changes taking place clearly indicates that we have entered a different world and as a result a different world of business and work. (See Table 1)

- Things are no longer necessarily linear (cause and effect may not necessarily be clear).
- Things can robustly and continuously change (what holds true today may no longer be so tomorrow).

- All possibilities are potentially true at all times (as explained by quantum science). "'Truth' is in the eye of the beholder". The framework (or context) of reference the beholder places around something determines the meaning he/she attaches. This may differ from the meaning somebody else attaches as a result of a different interpretation of context.
- Multiple realities are constantly playing themselves out around us simultaneously. A response to this can become more and more challenging as the number of realities we have to deal with increase. At an elementary level there are at minimum three realities at play at the same time - the perceiver's reality, the communicator's intended reality, the reality of the "space within which it gets communicated" (the context within which things are communicated).

  A simple context can become potentially very dynamic, but at the same time also that much more problematic and complex due to the differences in perception of reality.
- Quick and continuous changes result in things becoming obsolete in a short space of time - systems, skills and knowledge, becoming quickly outdated adding to the concept of "fads". Fads could well have been valuable knowledge at some point in time, but has become outdated due to the changed definition of context and meaning around it.
- The total space around us and around organizations in particular, is richly endowed with a network of possible linkages and relationships. Within this potential chaos of endless linkages and possibilities, there seems to emerge an order of meaning that makes it easier for

certain individuals, economic networks, and organizations (or groups thereof) to interface with one another. These orders of meaning are born from a "common understanding" of the "space" or context around them. From these contexts challenges are borne that call for appropriate action or response. Understanding the context and responding appropriately may result in success. Not understanding and not responding appropriately very often result in failure.

Many more changes can be highlighted and discussed in depth. This is however not the intent of this book. What is clear is that these changes have resulted in organizations having to deal with increasing emerging levels of uncertainty and ever increasing complex contexts. This has often resulted in people finding themselves at a loss in this ever changing landscape and as a result finding it difficult to plan for the future in organizations. This has resulted in the "chaos disciples" believing that longer term future planning is not possible anymore. Some voices of sanity prevailed during this chaos debate. They were closely aligned with natural science principles in identifying the patterns of consistency in the world of continuous change around us.

In this apparent chaotic landscape, patterns of consistency can be observed, be it in a formal organization or in a self-organizing environment. When left to self-organise, a pattern along very clear themes of consistency will emerge. These themes, with its fractal patterns, manifest across the full spectrum of organizations, from the less complex to the more or advanced complex.

Table 1

BROAD TRENDS IN GLOBAL SYSTEMS

Simple Systems — Up to the 60's – linear economies	Late 1960 – 1980's: Chaos theories dominated with emergence of complexity thinking	Complex Systems — 1990's – early dawn of complexity in quantum non-linear thinking
Predictable – the future is a continuation of the past		Volatile with multiple surprises – "the future is not what it used to be"
Change requires a recipe that can be used elsewhere		Same recipe often results in the wrong answer – change is not linear
Gathering skills/knowledge will help you to add value		Contextually appropriate knowledge and skill assist in adding value
Answers and principles were Absolute		Nothing is absolute anymore – Everything is relative
Stability is a given	Instability / chaos is a given	There are patterns of stability within instability
Hierarchies are based on seniority, status, numbers, qualifications		Hierarchy is based on context, complexity and value add
Life is linear		Life is linear and circular and Diagonal and retro, and....
Silent and boomers		X, Y, Z
Central, control, hierarchy, etc		Dispersed, facilitate, value,

© Pieter Marais - 2001

To effectively deal with these patterns of consistency, there is a growing realisation that capabilities other than skills and knowledge are essential to deal with these patterns of complexity or context, within or outside of organizations. It calls for a core capability to generate meaning from chaos despite the dynamic changes in skills, knowledge and experience, or even in the absence thereof, to deal with the challenges of context we find ourselves in. This deep capability to generate contextual understanding results in appropriately aligned action to address the challenges of increasing contextual complexity.

Contextuality, which implies the ability to understand and deal with context is becoming and will continue to become an increasingly important factor discerning successful from non-successful companies. It will set companies that move with the times apart from those companies that stagnate.

Contextuality increasingly becomes a clear differentiator. It also brings a different dynamic to global community, societies, organizations and individual people. Companies understanding this and appropriately dealing with this in all facets of its business are the ones more likely to ensure a longer-term sustainable future. This applies to societies, communities and individuals a well.

Despite the volatility of the world we live in, nothing can be left to chance anymore as the future is no longer an extrapolation of the past. Within the volatility we find ourselves in, there are these patterns of contextual consistency mentioned earlier. The ability to understand these patterns and to use them in setting up, positioning, stratifying strategies, to mention some of the more important ones, will differentiate the flexible and agile companies from the rest. These patterns of consistency in contexts need to be understood to enable appropriate response.

At more complex and uncertain contextual levels scenario building becomes, for example, vital to chart a course for the future. This will assist in defining the variables and changes in variables that indicate when an alteration in course is necessary. At less complex levels the focus may be on ensuring that we continuously improve on what we do, as the game plan of our industry may be just about that and nothing more. Knowing these contexts and knowing how it needs to be played, enable a more appropriate response towards the challenges a company faces. If not managed contextually appropriate (from the appropriate contextual level) for coherent value add, the robust dynamics can obstruct and even result in a destruction of value, making an organization vulnerable to the challenges and threats of its environment.

Contextuality a natural phenomenon

Key Points:

1. *Contextuality is a natural order found in all open systems.*
2. *Some life systems, e.g. social systems and business systems are actively interfered with skewing the natural ordering process.*
3. *Knowledge of contextuality and the active managing thereof are important to neutralise the skewing and to facilitate the value adding qualities of the natural contextual layering of open systems like organizations.*

Elliot Jaques, with Stratified Systems Theory, made the initial breakthrough identifying and describing natural layers of context. A number of researchers, consultants and practitioners, through their own organizational exposure, author included, moved the understanding of these layers of context and complexity to a new depth. What has become clear is the generic nature and transportability of these levels. No matter where in the world one goes the contextual theme of work remains constant. This has led researchers and practitioners to appreciate the natural order of context and complexity that exists.

To try and explain the principle of context and the natural layering thereof, one can use a salad dressing as a concrete analogy. When thinking about a salad dressing people tends to consider the "integrated" mix, no-one really considers the layers of its content. When shaken up, the layers integrate and create the liquid substance that adds flavour to a salad. Left to stand for a while, a natural process of settling down will result in visible layers of fluid and matter. In nature there are clear layers of order from the elementary to the more complex. Even in society these natural layers of order can be identified. There seems to be a clear pattern of natural layers of order, or natural layers of value add. Understanding these layers, what they consist of and how they interface are what contextuality in essence is about.

The interesting notion is that no matter how these layers are mixed up in organizations, over time, *if left untouched*, a natural layering will emerge. This layering in an organization may be a manifestation of the organization's responses to its context. It may also be a manifestation of what happens in the organization as a result of the capability or incapability of its leadership or employees to deal with the context of challenges facing the organization. In today's world, however, we do no longer have the luxury of waiting for natural processes to take its course. Natural order is actively interfered with which demands the need to understand orders of context and how to change, manage and mobilise it for value. For this reason understanding context and how this translates into the organizational aspects of positioning, design, structure, etc., is becoming vital to ensure appropriate intent, strategy and design to affect the appropriate and desired outcomes. It is becoming vital for competitiveness, sustainability, viability and relevance for the present as well as the future of organizations. If not understood and deliberately mobilised, risks to company increases dramatically as the company "sails blindly" and often becomes victim to circumstance resulting in reactive response or sometimes demise.

What is contextuality?

> **Key Points:**
>
> 1. Multiple factors contribute to a differentiation of less versus more complex contexts.
> 2. There are seven clearly definable themes or layers of context.
> 3. Within each of these contexts (themes) there is also a progression of complexity.
> 4. These contexts are not a linear progression where the next is more of the same of the previous.
> 5. There are quantum order changes from one context to the next.
> 6. One level (or context) is not more important than the other. Each context is important as each contribute significantly different value.

There is no simple definition of context or contextuality due to its multi-faceted nature. Context deals with:

- The degree of certainty/uncertainty of what needs to be done;
- The degree of certainty/uncertainty of the environment and the dynamics thereof, that needs to be dealt with;
- The degree of availability/non-availability of information to respond to challenges;
- Whether actions that need to be taken are based on facts or assumptions;
- Whether what needs to be done requires someone to do as told, or whether it requires the development of frameworks and models for action;

- The time it will take to reach the point of evaluation whether you are on track, or not, in delivering on what you set out to do;
- The ambiguity, depth, trend and theme of the multiple factors that makes up a specific context.

These elements and many more assist in defining the contexts of meaning and nature of value add. Within this contextual debate it becomes clear that:

1. There are different levels of context, each one significantly different from the other;
2. There is an order of increasing complexity of these contexts;
3. This "increase in order" also implies that each consecutive context adds a different value to the full picture;
4. One level of context is not more important than the other but each context's value add is a quantum different from the next level up or down;
5. The more complex the context, the more variables with more uncertainty, less clarity, less information and even the need to develop frameworks and models for understanding, needs to be dealt with.

Contextuality, the extension, elaboration and further advancement on Elliot Jaques' Stratified Systems, is a framework for understanding, defining and dealing with these increasing contexts of complexity in society in general and more specifically so within organizations. The existing and growing body of knowledge has become much more sophisticated and effective in dealing with the debate regarding context and complexity and more specifically context and complexity in organizations.

Contextuality – the "fundamental structure" ("DNA") of life systems: Society, business, work, people

---

Key Points:

1. *There are 7 clearly identifiable quantums of context irrespective of the level of sophistication of a society.*
2. *Some, not all, of these quantums of context can be found in organizations depending on the challenge an organization needs to deal with.*
3. *The nature of contextual challenge will determine the nature of organizational response and in effect the number of contextual layers appropriate to deal with the challenge.*
4. *People vary in their capacity to generate meaning and add appropriate contextual value. This can be determined and therefore appropriately mobilised.*

Contextuality is very relevant to the world in general and the world of work, in particular, today. It has moved beyond the theory debate and has moved towards a science of organizations and people that can even be quantified. The quality of organizational strategies, activities, interventions, people capability to deal with context, to name a few, can be expressed in a quantified value that will facilitate deliberate discussion, selection and action to affect appropriateness. This will also raise the quality of debate, strategy and people.

The framework emerged through being totally involved with business, organizations and people over a period of more than 40 years. The depth of understanding has resulted in an appreciation, starting with Elliot Jaques's SST and moving into Contextuality, that have brought us to the point to appreciate that we are working with the "fundamental structure" of the context of work and work contextual understanding of people. The findings are based on consistent patterns found globally in different economies, societies, cultures and amongst employees within companies as well as entrepreneurs outside of the formal business environment.

1. Work across the global environment demonstrates very clear consistent clusters of themes irrespective of the country or industry and irrespective of the level of sophistication of the economy, government or people. These themes manifest in seven quantum contexts of growing complexity described in more detail later in this book.

2. People demonstrate consistent themes or patterns of contextual capacity in dealing with these contexts - manifesting as an internal capability to generate meaning in context.

3. This capability develops and grows at a highly predictable rate over time, something Elliot Jaques has postulated and which after decades and through thousands of practical organization and individual data has been confirmed at very high levels of predictability.

This has led to the conclusion that we are dealing with this "fundamental structure" of work and people. This "fundamental structure" makes the difference between excellence or mediocrity, success or failure. Contextuality, this "fundamental structure" of societies, organizations and people, is based on broad principles of SST and general complexity science. Contextuality considers the clusters of increasing complexity. It layers the world and more specifically the world of work into quantum domains of increasing "complexities of *value add*". The focus of contextuality is on the different levels of context and the "value-add" thereof, not on factors like "hierarchy of reporting, importance, size of reward, position in the company, grading of roles, or title". It even takes a robust step towards quantifying the quality of value delivery. In this way quality of value becomes even more appropriately contextualised.

The inclusivity of contextuality

Key Points:

1. *Contextuality does not stand in competition with other models, be it business, management, social, scientific, or any other models.*
2. *The power of contextuality is in its inclusion and appropriate contextualisation, for appropriate value-add, of other models.*
3. *Contextualisation is a CONTEXTUAL framework describing the nature of value add, not a detailed content related model that gives the methodologies towards delivery of value add. Any other model can be incorporated or accommodated to facilitate the appropriate contextual contributions, providing it addresses the contextual challenges at the appropriate level.*

Where traditionally a number of models fight to stand alone or be recognised as "the most important" or "only real model of value" in the market, contextuality accommodates, integrates and contextualises other models. It is unique in the sense that it does not compete and do not need to compete with any other model. It is the framework that definitively defines the nature and scope of the playing field. It provides the justification for the existence and inclusion of other models and has the ability to contextualise these models for their appropriate value-add at the appropriate level of context and complexity.

The contextual choice of organizations

Key Points:

1. *Organizations theoretically have an inherent capacity to adapt naturally to contextual challenges.*
2. *Despite this theoretical ability, as a result of the:*
   - *fast pace of impact of contextual challenges,*
   - *the deliberate manipulation of the natural contextual structural alignment of the organization through inappropriate design, systems and practices, management philosophy,*

   modern organizations need a deliberate and focussed intervention to assist the organization to function as close as possible to the required natural layers of context and contextual value add its context demands.
3. *Organizations having the knowledge and capacity to facilitate a value adding and appropriately aligned contextual design and setup will more likely be the successful organizations with more appropriately empowered people.*

> 4. Organizations having the contextualisation knowledge and knowhow will have the capacity for a more appropriate approach towards e.g.:
> - Positioning and mobilisation for strategic value;
> - Operational enhancement and value delivery;
> - Setup and company design;
> - Utilisation of their human and other resources.

Organizations, if left completely undisturbed, will manifest and mature the layers of contextuality naturally, similar to our earlier salad dressing example. This is why organizations are referred to as being Complex Adaptive Systems (CAS). CAS refers to the capacity of a system to adapt naturally to its context or environment. However, organizations as social systems are never left to their own devices and multiple impacts deliberately or unintentionally are made on it. In this process organizations lose their capability and flexibility to adjust **naturally**. That they still adapt is true, but natural adaptation is difficult as a result of it being interfered with. They tend to lose this flexibility as a result of, for example, not being allowed to pitch at the right levels. This inhibition can be as a result of appointing the wrong people with the inappropriate contextual capability to deal with the challenges, thereby skewing the capacity of the organization to align and respond to the required contextual complexity challenges. It can also be interfered with as a result of inappropriate systems and policies being implemented, e.g. a rigid and inappropriate decisions framework. Operational decisions may be pulled up too high up the hierarchy inhibiting appropriate authority to act and add value of people at the operational levels. This may result in a loss of flexibility and an inappropriateness of value-add as a result of introducing systems/processes/structures/ interventions to the organization that does not "fit the required context" the organization needs to adapt to. This may also result in structures and accountabilities that do not enable the organization to meet its contextual challenges. There are numerous examples of enabled as well as disabled organizations that came about as a result of its appropriateness or inappropriateness in dealing with external or internal contextual challenges.

To leave organizations, especially in the modern fast pacing world in which we live in today, to mature and settle by itself, or to leave appropriately pitched intent and strategy "to chance" is unfortunately no longer desirable. Too many people and circumstances impact at too rapid a rate, sometimes artificially so, on the natural adaptive capacity of organizations. To enable the natural value-adding qualities of the contextual framework requires a knowledgeable choice. This choice should be based on a clear understanding of context to which an organization needs to respond to, as this will guide intent, strategy and appropriate design. This deliberate decision and action is necessary as the "nature" of self-organizing has been and continues to be interfered with. It is no longer possible for it to self-correct and adapt and a deliberate choice for relevance, that will guide further contextually appropriate action, is therefore a necessity.

An even more critical choice organizations needs to make and action, upfront, is whether they want to apply the principles of contextuality, this "fundamental structure" ("DNA") of organizations, to the organization. The choice is critical and the implications far reaching into all aspects of the organization and organizational life. It is fascinating to remember that any organization already has this in their "DNA" but needs dedicated attention to make it work as a business tool. The mere presence thereof in organizational "DNA" enables leaders and managers to mobilize this. In its current form it may be critically skewed as a result of multiple external and internal organizational impacts resulting in "contextual ineffectiveness and/or inefficiency". A pre-requisite for its mobilization is for leaders and managers to understand the different layers of contextuality and its value add thereby mobilizing from a platform of informed and knowledgeable choice.

It is important for organizations to choose whether contextuality is the organization and business framework or not. If the choice is made not to, there are certain implications that arise as a result of the increased risk of inappropriate contextualisation. The organization:

1. May not be appropriately positioned in the market;
2. May not be pursuing the appropriate business strategies;
3. May not be able to mobilize and realize its full capacity in terms of opportunity, growth, advancement and delivery;
4. May probably not achieve its optimal financial, profit, cost targets consistently;
5. May probably remain a bit of a lame duck as it may never even realize its potential to do better;
6. May not be geared, from a work and structural perspective, to deal appropriately and comprehensively with challenges;

7. May not understand the contextual capability of its people and their potential frustration as a result of their underutilization or over-extension with its resultant impact on motivation and value generating contributions;

8. May therefore run the risk of losing key skills and people;

9. May become one of the surprised or demised companies as a result of a lack of appropriate contextual response to the business challenges.

In certain organizations the more or less of achieving the above, despite not dealing appropriately with contextuality, may still be possible by chance, or by the by chance "appropriate" contextual capable leadership that could have emerged. Lack of consistency may however be an issue going forward and this will, more likely, reflect in performance inconsistency.

If on the other hand an organization does decide to embark on this as their business and organizational framework, there will be some clear impacts and implications, e.g.:

1. There may be an appreciation and understanding of the appropriately required pitch of the organization in the market;

2. There may be a better chance of putting appropriate strategies in place to realize the strategic market and organization intent and pitch of the business;

3. There may be a clear understanding of what design, in terms of contextual roles, structures, systems, the organization needs to put in place to realize the strategies and intent;

4. The chances of putting the right people with the right contextual capability in place to realize the requisite contextual value will be immensely enhanced;
5. There will be clear frameworks for organization as well as people development along the lines of value delivery, thereby saving time, energy and cost, often wasted in inappropriate frameworks e.g. inappropriate training;
6. It may result in the establishment of an appropriate, mature culture of value-add and accountability, with appropriately mature management and leadership philosophies and practice.

These are just some of the benefits to the organization. This will be further elaborated on in the book dealing with the organizational value of contextuality.

Why Contextuality is important to organizations

Key Points:

1. *Contextuality is a comprehensive framework for defining context and providing principles on the nature of content required to deliver appropriate value. (See water mass example quoted below).*
2. *It defines the nature and scope of organizational response to context, be it operation, market, national, etc.*
3. *This result in the understanding and determination of organizational pitch with resultant more appropriately aligned strategies, setup and design to enhance the potential for successful delivery on strategy, be it operational or company strategy.*

> 4. *This assists in determining appropriate models per level as support mechanisms towards success.*
> 5. *It enables the determination of the appropriate calibre of people to deal with the contextual challenges, increasing an organization's chances of success.*
> 6. *It facilitates organization wide coherence and alignment of intent, strategy, design, systems and people.*

Over and above the pros and cons mentioned above as well as comments regarding the relevance to the new paradigm of business, Contextuality:

1.   Defines and positions company contexts:

- Company pitch. A deep understanding of the dynamics of the environment the company needs to respond to, its market, its national contexts, its competitive realities and more, will result in clarity regarding company pitch. Contextuality therefore creates the context of meaning with clarity about the nature of depth and complexity thereof. In this process of understanding the use of various process methodologies, of which scenario building, scenario analysis and strategic planning is a critical element, will assist in understanding the context that determines the required pitch. Pitch implies that the company may have a variety of options available to it in the way it can and/or should respond. A company can decide not to play the national agenda of the country but to merely focus on the dynamics of the market being a market competitor. It may alternatively decide to consider competition merely in terms of generating profit better, faster, cheaper than competitors through innovative production practices. A deliberate choice about how the company should focus manifests from the clarity about the contextual pitch it should address. Understanding pitch has multiple implications for focus, structure, systems, quality of people, but above all increasing the likelihood of success and appropriate value-add.

- Company strategies. Understanding company pitch will assist in crystallizing the appropriate strategies to realize the pitch. In this way context and pitch will provide a clear framework for designing and honing of strategies appropriate to the context and the appropriately required pitch of the business of the organization. In this way it focuses company energy and efforts towards that which should be making a difference to company profit, sustainability, growth, expansion or even contraction and downscaling. In this way strategies become aligned to context and pitch and increase the likelihood of success and relevance of the company.

2. Assists in the definition of the requisite, optimal and appropriate contextual structure for realizing context and pitch.
   - Requisite process design.
   - Requisite roles that enable value delivery to context.
   - Requisite structures design to meet pitch/intent and strategy.

3. Provides the context for appropriate inclusion and contextualization of:

    - Models, frameworks, interventions – ensuring its contextually relevant application for value at the appropriate contextual level as well as facilitating the required deliverables and value add to the company;
    - Systems - for its appropriateness of support in facilitating the appropriate contextual delivery;
    - People - the appropriate deployment of their capabilities to deal with context and its complexities and to add the relevant value at the appropriate levels of context and complexity;
    - Stratification and pitch of People Development to ensure the enabling of people, aligned with company pitch and strategy, for realizing company value add.

This emphasize again that "Contextualisation" is an inclusive approach. It accommodates, includes and contextualizes most, if not all, current, emerging and still to emerge models of society, organizations and work. It decodes the "DNA" thereof to help understand where and how value is created or destroyed through appropriate and/or inappropriate contextual applications.

These are just some examples of the numerous applications and implications of the framework. The emphasis is on "contextual framework" of VALUE ADD.

Contextual framework can be further simplified and explained as follows:

It is the creating/defining/establishing of the <u>framework of meaning and the scope of thinking and action</u> (the nature of a mass of water).

A major dam differs significantly in context, intent and content from a splash pool. An ocean in turn differs significantly in context, intent and content from a dam. All three has a different contextual framework. The intent of the splash pool does not allow for sharks to be introduced into the pool. The intent of an ocean also does not allow for the introduction of a chlorine container and it probably will also not have any significant impact on the "inner workings" of the ocean.

The same principles apply to the world of business. Being clear about business context and intent has significant implications for organizational setup. Context gives clarity, determines and even drives content. Context therefore informs:

- <u>The positioning of the company;</u>
- The <u>nature of value</u> that must be added;
- The nature of <u>strategies, issues and dynamics</u> that needs <u>to be addressed;</u>
- The <u>nature of managerial and specialist work</u> that must be performed and as a result...
- The nature of the <u>required structure;</u>
- The <u>nature of as well as alignment of systems, skills and knowledge</u> to support the above.

The contextual framework and practices effectively creates/enables an integrated and coherent approach for appropriately addressing the increasing complex challenges (stratified complexity) an organization faces in its quest towards generating value due to the appropriate stratification of attention to detail. Appropriate stratification refers to the appropriate understanding of the business context, appropriateness of positioning and pitch of this context for appropriate value add, with the subsequent appropriateness of roles, delivery, structure, systems and even the culture that contributes towards clearly defined and appropriate accountability frameworks. It clearly moves away from defining work in terms of status, pay, grading, and non-value adding chains of command. Aspects like status, inappropriate chains of command and very specifically grading systems dates from the economies of the 60's and has no real alignment with the world of work today where flexibility and being nimble to challenge context with an appropriate pitch is first prize.

It is important to remember that the alignment or lack of alignment (be it conscious or not) between the contexts of societies/environments/markets/objectives and the contextual design of organizations in setting themselves up, more often than not, determines and/or explains the organization's potential for competitiveness or its lack of competitiveness and even demise. Knowledge of and deliberate design for contextual appropriateness is vital for current and future relevance and sustainability of companies.

Contextuality, SST and alignment

It is impossible to capture everything on Contextuality, SST, their associated processes, implications and applications in organizations in a book. It will take a continuously evolving library to deal with it all. It is only by working through and with the knowledge of the contextual levels, that the multiple dynamics of application and implication become clear. This booklet is geared towards sharing enough knowledge on contextuality and contextual levels, looking at organizations and societies through contextuality's lenses, to establish a continuous debate in organizations. This will assist organizations to achieve closer alignment between its "given" imperatives and its decided intent for future development, sustainability and success.

Contextuality refers to "The golden threat of Organizations". (See figure 1). Contextual alignment refers to:

- challenges stemming from the organization's context (especially those outside the organization) that
- must be adequately addressed to ensure contextually appropriate organizational deliverables which
- implies that the organization must ensure that at minimum it matches its intent, design and setup, with the contextual challenges that could determine its success or failure.

By implication it requires the organization to ensure appropriateness in the pitch of its intent and strategies and the capacity of its people to adequately develop and address the appropriate pitch and strategy. When intent, strategy and capacity under-pitches, there is the danger of losing the edge. If it over-pitches there is the possibility of making it too difficult and complex to maintain. However, if successfully pitched and acted upon, it can make it exceedingly difficult for competitors to keep up.

When context is clear, other alignments also come in to play to support the appropriateness of pitch. These alignments are the aspects within the arrow point area of the picture below. These must be aligned to support the golden threat or else the organization runs the risk of a:

- lack of coherence,
- lack of consistency,
- lack of appropriateness of aspects like structure, roles and accountabilities.

that will impact negatively on organizational performance and delivery.

Figure 1

Organisation and Work in Context

The Golden Thread in Organisations: Context, Delivery, Pitch

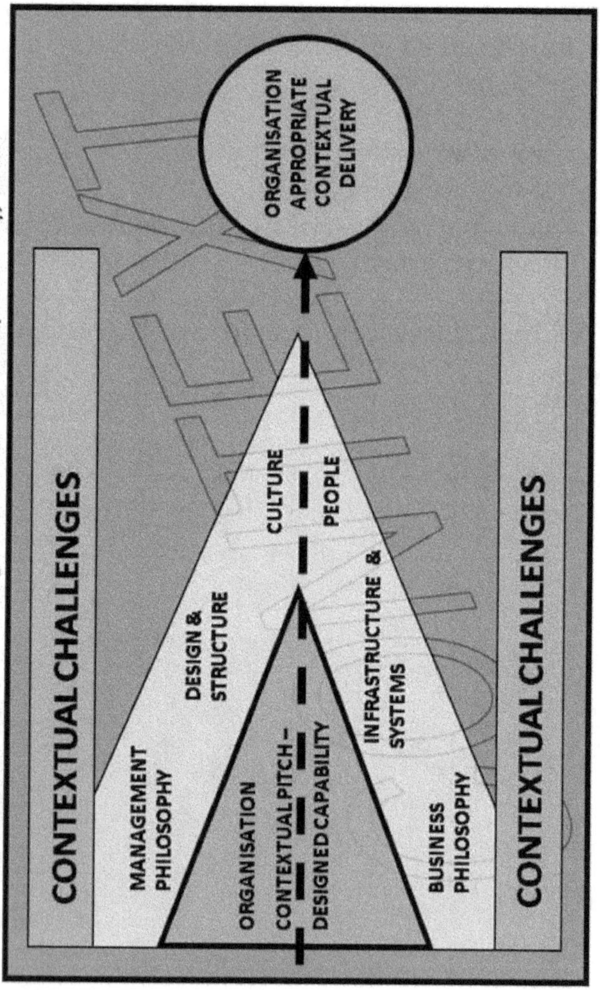

CONTEXTUAL CHALLENGES

CONTEXTUAL CHALLENGES

MANAGEMENT PHILOSOPHY

DESIGN & STRUCTURE

CULTURE

PEOPLE

ORGANISATION CONTEXTUAL PITCH – DESIGNED CAPABILITY

INFRASTRUCTURE & SYSTEMS

BUSINESS PHILOSOPHY

ORGANISATION APPROPRIATE CONTEXTUAL DELIVERY

©Pieter Marais Adapted from: E. Jacques – The Requisite Organisation - 1989

Comprehensive contextual understanding is a prerequisite for understanding and defining appropriate (requisite) delivery. Requisite delivery defines in turn requisite pitch of the appropriate delivery. Pitch defines the nature of needed capability, the nature of appropriate supportive structures, systems, management philosophy, as well as knowledge, skills and competency make-up for appropriate delivery.

The value chain of context, complexity and value-add (See figure 2)

Contextuality is the framework that assists in defining context and the nature of delivery. It is effectively a **value chain of work, organizations, context and the requisite value add**. It is NOT a hierarchical system of importance, grading, pay, etc. It does give clear principles and guidance for appropriate company design and structural setup to ensure requisite performance and value-add delivery.

Figure 2

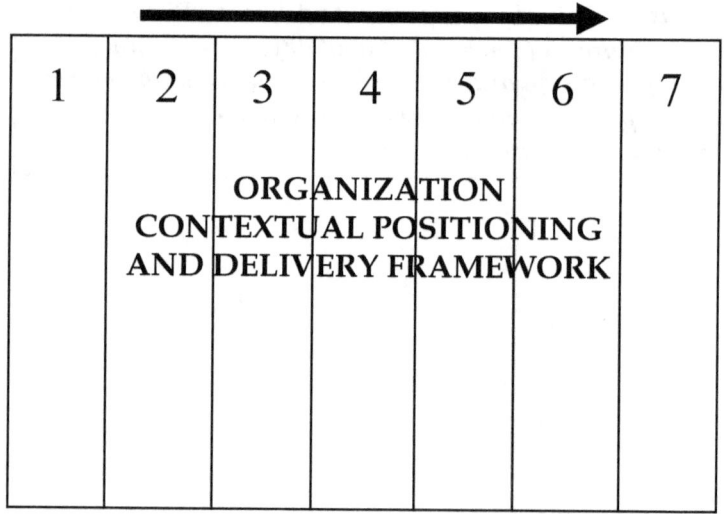

CONTEXTUAL VALUE-ADD

1	2	3	4	5	6	7

ORGANIZATION
CONTEXTUAL POSITIONING
AND DELIVERY FRAMEWORK

© Pieter Marais 2001

Some basic principles of Contextuality (advanced SST) (See figure 3)

Overlaps

Seven levels of complexity have been defined. These levels are globally transportable. Some, not necessarily all of them, can be observed in business and life domains in every part of the world. In certain economies it may be more or less sophisticated, but the general nature of the theme remains constant.

Levels 1 to 3 are broadly referred as the operational domains of an organization. Levels 3 to 5 are broadly referred to as the organizational domain, while levels 5 to 7 is referred to as the systemic domain. It is clear that at levels 3 and 5 overlaps take place. (See figure 3).

This implies that at level 3 both operational and organizational interests are considered – loosely referred to as the strategic-operational domain. At level 5 the focus is on both the organization and the broader systemic context around it. Reference to the broader systemic implies the direct involvement in co-designing political, economic, social, wider industry issues of a country or the larger economic region (Mercosur, NAFTA, SADEC, etc.) within which the industry and therefore the organization needs to be positioned.

Figure 3

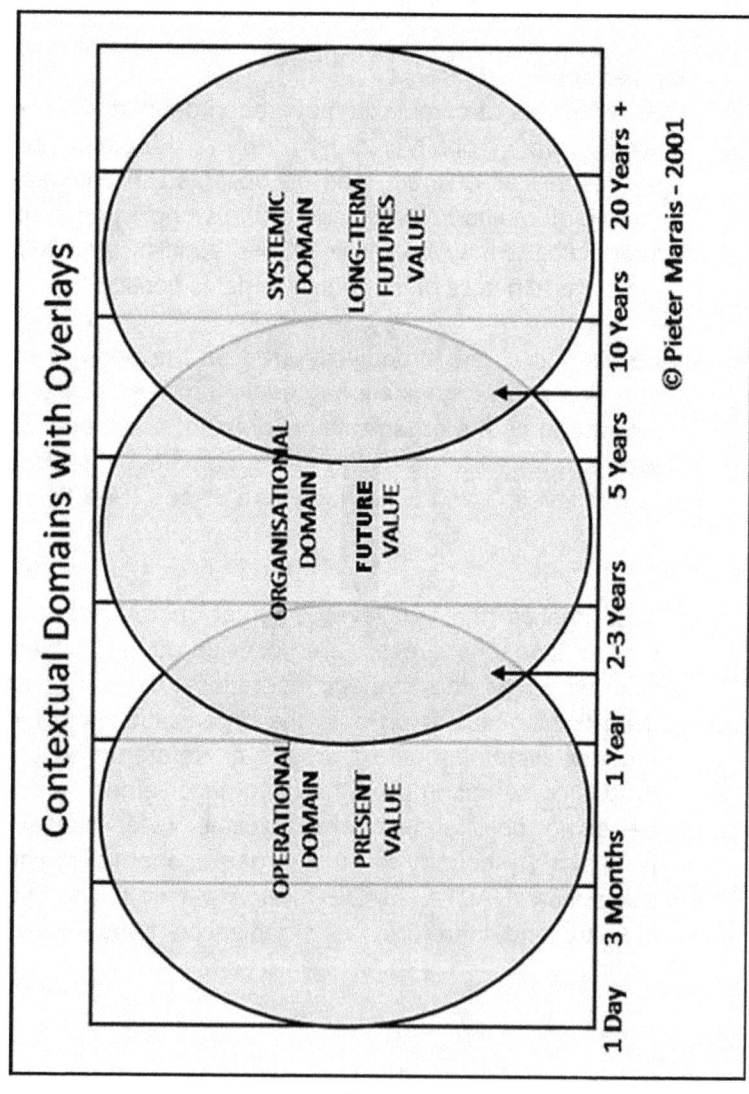

Contextual Domains with Overlays

OPERATIONAL DOMAIN — PRESENT VALUE

ORGANISATIONAL DOMAIN — FUTURE VALUE

SYSTEMIC DOMAIN — LONG-TERM FUTURES VALUE

1 Day | 3 Months | 1 Year | 2-3 Years | 5 Years | 10 Years | 20 Years +

© Pieter Marais - 2001

Timeframes

Key Points:

1. *Contextual timeframe of discretion deals with the time span from the point of initiation to the point of evaluation.*

Jaques refers to timeframes of work. (See figure 3). It is important to understand what timeframes we refer to. Timeframes can refer to the time from starting up (point of initiation) to the point of completion. It can also refer to the time from initiation to the point of evaluation whether something is on its way of becoming successful or not. The timeframe we refer to in contextuality is the latter - the time it takes from initiation to the point of evaluating whether the process has the potential to eventually deliver, or is on route towards achieving objectives.

Although it may carry a sense of the full time horizon, it does not refer to timeframe of thinking and also not the timeframe towards completion. A person may think in 5 year time horizons but effectively acts and puts in place something of which the appropriateness, or not, of direction or value will show up in a 2 year period (not completion yet), which implies that the role most probably tends to fall in the level 3 domain, PROVIDING THAT it does deal with the level 3 themes. Timeframe is **not** the qualifier of the level of the role. The actual THEME OF THE WORK AND THE NATURE OF THE VALUE ADD CONTRIBUTIONS of a role, when compared to the contextual (SST) framework, determines the actual "pitch" or the role.

A practical example from the mining industry can be used to demonstrate the timeframe principle. Often geologists see their work as dealing with the "Life of mine" – which refers to the "looking forward" over the mine's 20 year plus lifespan. However, on closer inspection the "life of mine" is a continuous process of adjustment. It requires the continuous gathering of information from geological investigations, production information, existing geological maps and the modelling of this data on existing computer programmes. The process tends to be shorter term and modelling of the ore body over time results in continuous adjustment. This whole exercise puts a number of the geological activities predominantly in the level 2 domain. So, despite the fact that there is a 20 year plus context of the future, the actual work, delivery and contribution takes place at level 2. This however, does not imply that certain geologists do not become involved in the level 3 and 4 domains nor does it take away from the fact that some of these geologists apply their knowledge and skills in direct concrete activity at level 1. Quite often geologists are required to apply their trained knowledge and skills in the concrete and daily activity of a mine – all focussed on the shorter than 3 months process.

The contextual levels

Key Points:

1. *The contextual levels explain the nature of the world around us, as well as the nature of work, better than any other known model, or framework, available to us.*
2. *Each of these levels is significantly different in context and content to one another. (See discussion under next heading). A next level is not merely an extrapolation, or merely more in size or number of the previous level.*
3. *Each level needs to be dealt with differently to extract the specific value-add thereof.*

The contextual levels are globally transportable. Not only does it explain the "DNA" of work wherever work gets done, it can also be used in a myriad of ways to determine, design, effect and explain why things should, are or have been happening in organizations as well as society at large. Contextuality in effect explains anything where people are involved – it explains social networks of which organizations are but one form. It is a framework against which dynamics and processes can be evaluated, decided and planned for impact and value. It can also be used as a framework to explain dynamics in process (the why of things) and even contextualise and explain historical events - therefore the reference to the "myriad ways of application".

Generic characteristics of contextual levels
- The **value add** from each level is significantly different.
- The **context and points of reference** of each level differs.
- The kind of **knowledge content** as well as processing thereof differs at each level.

- **Skills and knowledge content within each level can vary from very elementary to highly advanced**. More advanced skills and knowledge does not equate to dealing with a more advanced context of complexity, it merely implies that the skills or knowledge necessary to deliver quality value add may be of a more advanced nature.
- The **contextual capability required** to deal with the challenges of each level differs significantly.

Each level therefore requires a **different processing of context and content** to facilitate **appropriate value add**. Each level therefore also differs in nature regarding the deliverable (output value add) that needs to be "put on the table".

The difference between context and content

Key Points:

1. *Context deals with the nature of intent (not impact), generic processes and framework of, for example, skills, knowledge, experience, models and value add required for appropriate delivery at each level.*
2. *Content deals with, for example, the actual appropriate skills, knowledge, experience and models required to mobilise for appropriate value add.*

The difference between context (complexity) and content (knowledge, skills, competence) must be briefly put under the spotlight. High levels of skilled/knowledgeable competence can be found at the less complex level 1 (this includes professional skills and knowledge in medical, financial, engineering, etc. environments). A high level of contextual thinking, on the other hand, does not necessarily equate a deep level of skills and knowledge competence.

People with less sophisticated training can be capable of dealing with highly complex contextual issues. However, training to enable the application of sophisticated knowledge and skill will enhance the richness of their contextual contribution and value-add. In terms of the nature nurture debate it implies that nature provides the hardware while nurture enables the maximisation of the "hardware". If opportunity for development, growth, exposure is maximised the possibility of maximising "hardware" is good. If on the other hand there is less opportunity for exposure, growth, development the hardware is not devalued, as the capability is still inherently in place, but the potential for maximisation is inhibited due to the lack of opportunity and exposure. At a point of early detection of this gap, the gap between contextual capability (hardware) and competence (as in skills and knowledge) can still be closed. A gap can also be the result of choice, beliefs and other. This domain will be covered in the book dealing with Contextuality and people.

An issue that always surfaces in grading structures of companies has to do with impact of decision-making as well as size of reporting structure. Size is a contentious issue in the contextuality debate. Size does not contribute to complexity, but merely refers to "more of the same" on a horizontal **content difficulty** level. Impact (which essentially is tied into a value judgement) does not play a role in the determination of, or change in the contextual complexity of work. It merely contributes to an understanding of the risks associated with work irrespective of whether it is at a low or high level of contextual complexity. Contextuality asks about the intent of doing. The intent gives a clear indication of pitch. Even at the less complex level, impact can potentially be far reaching but never intended and never planned for. Timeframe of intent may focus on a reasonably short period. A product or process may come about as a result of wanting to solve a gap at level 2. It may eventually, over time, reach the far corners of the globe without being the initial intent. The mere fact of "going global" does not necessarily imply advanced complexity. These will be dealt with in more depth in the book "Contextuality and Organizations".

Contextuality's (advanced SST's) view on some of these "holy cows" in companies moves the game plan away from traditional ways of determining value. Contextuality asks the fundamental question about "VAUE ADD" to company. It also challenges various aspects of current organization setup and design, as well as a company's' views of the world. The world is moving, albeit slowly, to a more contextual rather than a content view. Content is not discarded, it is in fact emphasised but emphasised in terms of contextual appropriateness. Mere acquiring of knowledge and skill is of limited use and value to companies. Knowledge and skill acquired to deliver enriched and contextually appropriate value is what differentiate winning companies from the "run of the mill" companies. Companies that identify and move timeously with these trends will become the winners of tomorrow.

Description of contextual levels

A systematic discussion of the levels will be followed in this document starting from what is referred to as level 1 or the least complex level, progressing through each level to the most complex level, level 7. It needs to be reiterated that depth of skill and knowledge within each context (level), potentially span a wide spectrum from non-educated to highly educated work. Even at level 1 you will find deep level expertise. Expertise may be connected to the depth of knowledge and skill and not necessarily to a more complex level of context.

The different levels can never be described in full, as the information per level will require volumes that also will need to be upgraded constantly. Only key concepts with underlying key principles will be discussed for basic understanding.

Task execution (©Pieter Marais 2003) – Contextual Complexity level 1

This level has everything to do with the actual performing of direct tasks and delivery of concrete and measurable results within a relatively short period of time. At this level knowledge, skill and experience is applied in the performance of the task as well as in the overcoming of direct obstacles to task achievement. Performance of tasks as well as obstacle elimination at this level often requires a reliance on sensory observation and immediate/short-term adjustments.

Context level 1 - Key characteristics:

- Application of trained/educated skills, knowledge and acquired experience to perform a task and deliver a concrete result in real-time, within days or weeks. Knowledge/skills/experience covers the spectrum from elementary work to deep expert applications.
- Success in the work requires a direct comparison of results with requirements to decide appropriateness and/or to effect immediate/short term action to achieve the required delivery. Skills, knowledge and experience form the basis for evaluation as well as changes that can/should be affected.
- Use clear task descriptions, guidelines and achievement specifications to judge how the "task at hand" needs to be approached.
- Using direct sensory observation to decide the appropriate quality and quantity of work. Feel, see, hear, taste, smell when things are not in line with expectations and take the necessary action to

ensure compliance.
- Changes made may consist of adaptation to direct process of executing a concrete task or the "tools" being used for task execution. At the "more complex" end of this level the rearrangement of the daily, weekly work schedules of the work team may also form part of the changes.
- Delivering the "right" quantity and quality of product, service or task within the required timeframe and within pre-determined specifications.
- Organise the work of a team ensuring that they know what to do and have what is necessary to do the work (material and clarity on timeframe and quality of delivery). The analogy is that of a playing captain – although he "leads"/organises the team he is still responsible for delivering and participating in the actual work to be performed.
- Time frame from initiation to evaluation of task/service/product delivery is usually within 3 months.

Context level 1 - Typical measurement areas/ measurements:

- Work delivered according to predetermined standards of quality, quantity and time e.g. daily production according to set standards of quality, quantity and time – successful task execution.
- Correct application and use of material, tools, technologies to ensure minimum waste.

- Daily, weekly, monthly organising of team activities around concrete task performance that ensures expected delivery.
- Correct application of knowledge, skills and experience in e.g. performing a required procedure or direct identification of what is "wrong", e.g. diagnosing that a patient has flu (based on knowledge, skills and experience in the here and now – short-term).
- Compiling information/data into an appropriate format and ensure the correctness thereof e.g. a correct set of financial statements.

Context level 1 – Typical kind of innovations:

- Direct concrete adaptation of material and tools to enable delivery on expected quality, quantity and timing of tasks more effectively.
- Direct concrete adaptation of immediate process and methodology of the task to enable optimal quality task delivery.
- Changes suggested and/or made to the short-term plan of work (daily, weekly) to ensure achievement of short-term quality, quantity and timeousness of work delivery.
- Changes suggested and/or made to work teams to ensure short-term quality, quantity and timeousness of work delivery.

Optimal delivery or service unit (©Pieter Marais 2003) – Contextual Complexity level 2

This level is essentially responsible for providing a comprehensive and detailed plan with the supportive wherewithal to enable a unit to appropriately and optimally deliver on objectives, be it production or service objectives. This implies planning for a period ranging between 3 months up to one year that will result in the achievement of objectives. Working towards the achievement of objectives also requires a constant focus on the optimization and improvement of the existing processes and systems to eliminate obstacles preventing performance and to also consider ways of enhancing objective achievement. This is clearly the focus domain for continuous improvement. Enhancing the processes and systems that will result in improvement of quality and quantity of objective achievement, its speed of delivery as well as improved cost is an important dimension at this level. Specialists use their advanced skill/knowledge to determine the origin and define the detail of problems and obstacles. Through specialist investigation and knowledge application solutions are developed which may involve re-engineering of aspects of existing systems, (re)design, (re)shaping and replacing of parts of systems and processes with new processes to ensure systems advancement and optimal delivery. The main objective is to remove obstacles and/or enhance/improve the ways (methods, processes) towards achieving objectives.

When considering intent, timeframe as well as core business process and value add, a huge amount of businesses find themselves in this space. Many consultancies and consulting related work feature at this level. Expert knowledge and services to assist in problem identification, solution development and continuous improvement are critical elements in value add at this level. Contextual capability also explains why these consultancies are populated by "clever young people" – something to be explained in more detail in next publications. Many businesses focused on service delivery may also "pitch" at this level.

Context level 2 - Key characteristics:

- Comprehensive planning of the process of production/service target achievement. This requires focussing on all aspects from start to completion of objectives achievement. Issues to address include amongst others:
  - Clearly laid out plans that will ensure target achievement over periods of up to one year, or achieving a position of evaluating the appropriateness, or not, of the direction and possible success, or failure, which may result in "pushing ahead", or having to re-plan.
  - A clear understanding of the required production/service outcome and how this fits into the overall business objectives.
  - The definition of objectives to be achieved, underpinned by clear task and parameters definitions of quality, quantity and time for delivery in the short to medium term.
  - Clarity as to how defined tasks, with their parameters, fit together as part of the comprehensive detailed service or production plan.

- o   Planning for the timeous availability of material, tools and technology for the work to be performed at level 1.
- o   Ensuring the availability of skilled/trained and motivated people and teams to do the work. This does imply knowledge of the team and their skills levels, the identification of gaps in knowledge, skills and experience that can potentially interfere with task delivery and steps being taken to close such gaps.
- o   Ensuring the appropriate ergonomic environment within which tasks need to be performed – be it air, water, light, safety, health, etc.
- o   Having available and in place processes for early alert on deviations from intended plan to enable timeous corrective action that will still ensure eventual overall target achievement. These will include for example:
    - ▪ Cost control systems to detect and correct deviations to ensure achievement within budget parameters smoothed out over a period of up to one year. This may result in months of over-expenditure for critical business reasons but with clarity as to how this will be smooth out to still ensure "coming in within budget".

- Detecting deviations from production or service targets and the investigation into origins of problems, developing of solution options.
- In the process people will apply their own as well as utilise other people's skills, knowledge and experience in resolving problems in delivery. Problems may include obstacles, blockages, design problems, inefficiencies in the processes of production or service, the supportive systems, the applied technology, the actual planning process, the logistics of supply of material to the production or service unit or products and services to the clients or users, etc. Skills, knowledge and experience will be used for:
  - o Research or investigation, can be undertaken in individual capacity, as a production/service team or as a project team, by utilising experts, to identify the need or problem and develop a clear understanding around it and how it impacts and prevents objective achievement or service delivery. This may lead to full scale research projects to delineate the full scope and definition of the problem, inefficiency, obstacles, and bottlenecks or needs and requirements.
  - o Research and development into solutions. It will start from the clear definition of the issues, doing further research to acquire the appropriate knowledge that will assist in the

development of appropriate solutions to defined problems or needs.

o Solutions may take the form of:
- Re-engineering parts of the process/technologies/systems that prevent or inhibit achievement.
- Off the shelve buying and implementation of existing technologies or solutions to enhance current processes and systems to improve delivery and results.
- Development of a programme or product that addresses customer needs and requirements.
- Developing unique first time in the world solutions to problems from existing sources of information. Although it is new, the intent and subsequent process is geared towards solving an existing problem. Innovative (never done before) problem solving is therefore a critical component at the higher end of this level.

- Responding to the needs or requests from customers. This response to needs may come about as a result of a needs analysis or research project on needs identification. A response may take the format of adjustment to existing services or needs, or the development of a product or service to respond to specific customer needs.
- The above is underpinned by a drive for continuous improvement. The focus on continuous improvement

at this level ensures that what is in place gets fully optimised in terms of its value add and is effective in ensuring better delivery and achievement – quicker, more cost-effective and improved in quality.

- Time frame from the point of starting towards the objective to the point of evaluation can be up to 1 year.

Context level 2 - Typical measurement areas/measurements:

- Production target achievement over 3, 6 and up to 12 months.
- Service target achievement.
- Manufacturing target achievement.
- Cost target achievement.
- Safety and health target achievement.
- Customer satisfaction.
- Appropriate delivery of expertise in solving problems or the implementation/introduction of technologies into the existing process/system that will result in improved and optimal delivery and cost efficiency. (Shaping what is there to be better – continuously improving on the overall designs that are in place to ensure maximum and improved delivery).
- Indirectly, share price attractiveness through production, service target achievements on a quarterly, six-monthly and annual bases.

- Optimal availability, utilisation and delivery of production processes/systems.

Context level 2 – Typical kind of innovations:

Doing research, investigation and development that will result in changes to existing systems in an incremental and "continuous improvement" way. The objective is focused around the maximized availability and performance of that which is in place even if it does imply re-designing certain elements thereof.

Blockages are removed; parts of processes or systems are redesigned, re-engineered or re-equipped with different technologies; methods of doing things are adapted or changed. Adaptations are often affected based on benchmarking of same or similar processes with other companies.

The key drive is to make sure that what is in place works better or is improved to enable maximum contribution (quality and/or quantity of service or product/production) at lowest expense (be it money, energy, effort, time).

Undertake an identification and delineation of customer requirements or needs and develop, or construct, appropriate customer solutions.

**Integrated business unit (©Pieter Marais 2003) –
Contextual Complexity level 3**

This level brings together and integrates all facets of a business to achieve business objectives (e.g. profit) as an integrated business system. This refers to the integrated complete value chain from where the business starts (where raw material and resources enters) to where it finishes (where products, services, waste, etc leaves) with all support services. It considers all aspects of the business:

- The work to be done with the integration of tasks, work processes, roles;
- Formal organizational issues e.g. structures, systems, finance, technology, policies and procedures, all required and appropriate support services and others;
- Informal organizational issues e.g. behaviour, values, culture, informal networks and communication processes and others;
- People – their skills, knowledge, experience, expectations – not only now, but also pro-actively that what the business may need as changes for business enhancement are planned.

It deals with the interrelations (interactions) as well as integration of all the above that needs to be achieved to enable delivery on expected business results. In the process of addressing the above, an individual at this level also needs to consider what "new things" can be introduced to provide additional performance and profit advantage. New knowledge and technology applications, not off-the-shelf solutions or mere solutions to existing problems, are developed for step change advancement. This results from the acquiring, integration, customization and extrapolation of various sources of existing bodies of knowledge and/or technology, from own, associated and non-associated industries, for own environments. The focus here is on the new and innovative for general business unit enhancement. New products, processes, systems and services (that maximize business core competences and resources) are developed at this level. I need to emphasize that development at this level no longer focuses on solving direct customer problems or developing something that solve problems in current processes, systems, services. The objective is the enhancement of profit objectives of the integrated business unit through maximizing all business resources through new developments that will fully maximize all resources capacity. It is not merely enhancement of what is already in place to do the same better, faster, cheaper (continuous improvement level II), but a replacement to do differently for significant advancement. It involves the replacing of complete process, products, etc. of the business value chain.

Context level 3 – Key characteristics:

- Integrate and manage a complete business value chain with its support services. This implies the value chain from where the business starts up to where the product/service leaves the organization – the complete production process and the support services.
- A full understanding of how all these different parts of the business link up to an integrated whole for advanced business delivery.
- Ensure the optimal design of the business value chain, optimal structure to support the value chain, as

well as determining the number/size and utilisation of business resources (people, technology, finance, systems/processes). Resources allocated for maximum Return On Investment (ROI) and profit generation.

- Establish the culture and behaviours that support the business unit's objectives.
- Determining the optimal business frameworks, models, philosophies, policies and practice.
- Consider capitalising on revenue/cost opportunities from the value chain through:
  - Having a range of possible growth opportunities. This could mean the development and introduction of new products within and adjacent to the existing product portfolio, brown fields expansions within existing operations in e.g. resources industries. Motivation of major business unit capital projects to capitalise on these new opportunities.
  - Considering synergy opportunities as well as integration of multiple parts of the value chain for optimal value. This could imply stopping certain products/services and introducing the new. It may also imply combining more than one service outlet, outsourcing certain parts of the unit services for better value return to the business.
  - Benchmarking of business unit performance on critical measures against competitors and finding appropriate ways of increasing benchmark

position on these critical measures – thereby providing competitive advantage. This could result in radical renewal or change of business.

- Introducing new products or services to the existing portfolio and maximising resource utilisation.
- Acquiring knowledge and technology and integrate and develop advancements for optimised or new growth.
- Immediate community involvement and shaping. Be aware of developments in the community, broader society, legislative changes, etc. that may impact on viability and sustainability of the business for timeous and pro-active "plans of action". Involvement in communities has the intent of developing a conducive environment for people in the community to be comfortable with the presence of business in their space.
- Develop technology/knowledge solutions for the business unit that will replace complete parts of the value chain or replace technologies and knowledge being used currently. This development requires the borrowing, adapting and integrating of existing knowledge and technologies from own industry (e.g. the gold mining industry), associated industry (e.g. platinum mining industry) and even non-associated industries (e.g. Space Industry) that, through its development and implementation, will result in a step change business (e.g. profit growth) achievement. This is not merely continuous improvement to what is

there through the introduction of "off-the-shelve" new technologies (level 2), but an active development from the integration of these various technologies and knowledge basis into something developed and customized for own business.

- Time frame from initiation to evaluation can be up to 3 years.

Context level 3 - Typical measurement areas/ measurements:

- Business profit and profit growth:
  - Enlargement thereof through new investment in the existing business framework – e.g. new product within the existing service offering suite;
  - Through the development and bringing on board of e.g. technologies, processes to enhance the profit objectives and optimal business performance;
  - ROI on capital investment – NAV optimisation.
- Sustainable profit margin of business.
- Sustainability and safety.
- Technologies incorporated that affect a step change in profit and business achievement.
- Share price attractiveness through e.g. ROI, profit, margin and dividend returns.

Context level 3 - Typical kind of innovations:

- No longer just continuous improvement to or re-engineering problems out of the existing systems but a replacing of significant parts of the value chain and systems or processes (Not acquiring mere off the shelve solutions. Buying an existing product and doing some fine-tuning during implementation to make it work better tends more towards level 2).
- Newly developed technological and knowledge systems brought together from the integration and extrapolation from own, associated and remote industries with the necessary customization for own industry. This could imply that NASA technology are acquired, adapted and customized for the Mining industry, or this knowledge and technology is used to develop technologies that can be used for new/advanced value add e.g. robotics in underground mining operations. Using existing knowledge to develop and "package" a new and innovative approach that will replace large systems in business.
- Not improving on that which is there to make the whole system better, but an innovative development and replacement that will have implications for total operation. This will have implications for the way the total operation function, the different departments in the business, the people, finance and other connected issues.

- New Management Practices are also identified, acquired and implemented with the necessary customisation. In the process of implementing these changes the complete business context with its interrelations is managed towards optimized and advanced value add.
- Mergers and acquisitions can even take place at this level as a means of amongst others growing bigger, making sure that a constant stream of output is guaranteed (e.g. as a means of ore-replacement (getting new ground to mine for the ones mined out) in the resources industry), utilizing existing resources better by running a particular business better due to having the knowledge base that can be applied to make it work better and render enhanced profits.

Competitive market/industry positioning, growth and influence. (©Pieter Marais 2003) – Contextual Complexity level 4

This level essentially deals with multi-business and multi-level integration within the context of an intended market positioning. Against the backdrop of a 5-year competitor and associated business future scenario, strategic positioning and company profitability is affected through e.g. sustainability, growth, expansion, contraction strategies. Issues that are dealt with at this level include:

- What market position to establish. What new business to develop, what existing business to close down and how to manage these with the existing towards an integrated, maintained and/or growing profitability ratio. This may result in strategies to deal with new acquisitions, new ventures, diversification activities/strategies, joint ventures, etc. (taking the lead from the national economic/industry environment at level 5). In essence dealing with macro business strategies that impact the market and industry position of a company. This is done against the backdrop of detailed scenarios of the business context into the future.

- Initiate and develop new knowledge with the subsequent development of technology that will result in and or support the strategic positioning and direction of the company. Specialist focus and involvement result in the development of new science applications, e.g. genetic engineering in agriculture, genetic engineering in medicine, etc. within the framework of the new science framework of genetics. This implies the development of the new knowledge and new scientific technology and technological applications, e.g. cloning animals within the framework of agricultural generic engineering.

- Lobbying government (local and where appropriate also national) to influence market, industry and legislative direction that may impact on industry and as a result company sustainability. It also implies lobbying governments regarding the development and use of new scientific applications.
- <u>Co-determining</u> the immediate business contextual environment that has relevance for company wellbeing e.g. local community forums, provincial forums, industry forums and others.

Context level 4 – Key characteristics:

- This level is essentially about competition and positioning. The nature and scope of market/industry positioning and influence. Deliberate decisions about the business's/company's stature and place in the market/industry.
- Devising of strategies to bring about the positioning intent. Strategies may then include amongst other:
  - The establishing of new business streams (establish new integrated business units as described above) for the growth of a multi-business, multi-level business through new business initiatives;
  - Appropriate and selective mergers and acquisitions, take-overs, joint ventures that will enhance the business portfolio in line with the strategic positioning intent;

- New Greenfields investments, upstream and/or downstream value chain integration and development strategies into business units;
- Business portfolio diversification;
- Closing non-profitable business or business no longer fitting the strategic portfolio.
- Integrating the new, the "in the process of closing down" business with the existing profitable ones and maintain a profitability ratio.
- Clear 5 year growth strategy (pipeline of new quantified investment opportunities) with consideration of mergers, acquisitions, joint ventures that fits company market positioning and portfolio intent.
- Acquisition, allocation, withholding or re-deployment of appropriate strategic resources throughout the multiple, multi-level business to maximize opportunities for contribution to total business or company profitability. This includes financial resources for investment, people and new technologies for market strategic positioning.
- Growth into new areas of revenue generation – diversification strategies.
- Market/industry shaping and influencing.
- Decisions about the development of new markets, new knowledge development and potentially the technology applications that can result in new business ventures being established.
- Regional community leadership, local and national political lobbying and influencing which could be

through industry lobby groups.

- Be critically aware of potential and real emerging regional/national issues that could impact viability and sustainability of the business. Ensure pre-emptive and timeous development of strategic responses to protect against potential risks or threats.
- Co-operative ventures with competitors regarding shared industry interests.
- Establish the framework for SBU values, behaviour and culture, which may imply:
  - Alignment with a larger group strategy thereby being the custodians and sponsors of group frameworks, business philosophies, models and initiatives;
  - Establishing the framework (as an independent business) and allow customisation to business (at level 3) within the defined framework.
- **New zero based** development of knowledge, technology and the application thereof for a new or an enhanced strategic position of company or the development of a particular scientific field. This implies the **development of the new, what is not known, not existing,** e.g. can genetic engineering bring a new dimension to the business we are in (knowledge and technology currently not existing). Not the development of new products that enhances and replace what is largely already there, which tends to take place in the level 3 and even 2 domains.
- Duration of time frame from initiation to evaluation can be up to 5 years.

Context level 4 – Typical measurement areas/ measurements:

- Market position of company vis-à-vis competitors with subsequent new business growth.
- Life and continuous viability of businesses within a region/country.
- Maintaining of SBU profitability and/or contribution ratio to company.
- Share price attractiveness through sound market positioning and portfolio growth strategies.
- New knowledge, supporting models, technology development and applications that establish, effect and secure a strategic value position for the company.

Context level 4 – Typical kind of innovations:

Strategic transformation of the business through the development of new knowledge, new technologies, designing and putting in place new business with all the required resources to maintain strategic integrity and coherence ,as well as integrated SBU profitability.

National systemic, regional economic block co-design/co-determination (©Pieter Marais 2003) – Contextual Complexity level 5

At this level the leader and/or leadership team steps outside their role as company representative only. Responsibility for industry as well as company is rolled up into taking responsibility for co-creating the systemic environment within which the industry, and as a result own company, is positioned. Through partnering with national government(s) and or regional economic blocks (e.g. SADEC, MERCOSUR, NAFTA, EU, etc.), non-government entities and private enterprise, or acting as sole entity interfacing with national political, environmental, social, legislative, (PESTLL) bodies, co-design an environment (nationally and/or economic region) conducive for longer-term sustainability and viability of the larger economy and national industries. This is not a domain for mere lobbying of government and national forums but the domain of active co-creation. Normal lobbying of government can take place at any level depending on the intent of interface, the nature of the issues to address and the objective to achieve. At this level however, deliberate co-design and not mere lobbying is a key deliverable. Furthermore, business sector development or demise (e.g. the manufacturing sector of the country) is orchestrated at this level for its relevance or non-relevance to the future of the country. The national agenda and its future is therefore upfront and on the table at this level. National investment, divestment and/or industry sector change/diversification are made in the context of the emerging future national PESTLL environment, not for market position but for industry and country position. Long-term (5 – 10 years) scenarios on countries are made within which country investment/divestment and/or sector diversification business decisions are made. Specialists at this level are instrumental in the emergence of new science frameworks (e.g. the person that was responsible for the emergence of the new science framework of genetics).

Context level 5 – Key characteristics:

- Co-determine/co-design the national and/or regional economic block (e.g. Sadec, Mercosur, etc.) agenda, debate and outcomes around, amongst other, the following domains:
  - Economic
  - Political
  - Social
  - Environmental
  - Legal
  - Industry
- Develop a clear understanding of the emerging national/economic regional environment and consider investment into or divestment from a region/country based on pre-empting, at minimum 5 – 10 years into the future, the industry impact (new or current) in creating and/or enhancing an integrated national/economic regional sustainable and competitive environment. This is appreciated within global contextual frameworks around markets, politics, value systems (social, environmental, etc.).

- Co-design implies the co-establishment of the integrated whole of the above and not just co-designing pieces of legislation or national policy. It focuses and considers the optimal integration and mix of the above themes into a national integrated whole – politically, economically, socially, etc.
- The pre-emption and timeous mitigation of risks to company of emerging structural changes in the national/economic regional debates the company operates within. This cover the economic, political, social, environmental, legal and national industry debates that shapes the future national/economic regional environment over the next 10 years. Risk mitigation can take on various forms, from divestment/investment, co-design of national systemic issues through formal forums or information channels of pressure and influence, to co-creation and establishment of a conducive context for investment and more.
- Based on co-design involvement, a point may be reached where recommendations regarding investment in or divestment from a region/country can be made. This is based on a pre-empted take on the 5 – 10 year emerging national scenarios.
- Investment may be pre-empted by the creating of a national presence and influence prior to investment. The Presence is mobilized to establish, through co-design, a conducive investment environment that integrates politics, economy, social environment, industry mix and national legal frameworks.

- Disinvestment may have been pre-empted by a prolonged period of attempts towards creating a conducive environment for continued investment.
- The emerging of a new field of science and scientific knowledge e.g. genetics. Within this framework, downstream research, knowledge and supportive technology development for application into specific areas e.g. genetic engineering's value to agriculture, can then take place at a level 4.
- Time frame from initiation to evaluation can be up to 10 years.

Context level 5 – Typical measurement areas/ measures:

- Securing a conducive environment that optimises the lifespan of major regional/country investments.
- Risk mitigation and value protection/enhancement within the context of pre-emptive national/regional economic systemic change.
- Share value through national economic and industry stature. This at times may even be interwoven with the image of the country within which the operation is based.

Context level 5 – Typical kind of innovations:

- Co-design of the larger national/economic regional systemic context inclusive of the PESTLL and industry dynamics.
- Shaping the organization to fit into and/or for fitness in the emerging context, and/or deliberately co-designing the context for economic, company and industry relevance.
- Emergence of new science frameworks.

Global systemic co-design (©Pieter Marais 2003) - Contextual Complexity level 6

This level takes responsibility for the co-design of the global systemic environment(s) through direct involvement and influence in global design forums. Taking the lead from emerging global philosophy and value frameworks (at level 7), this level is intrinsically involved in the design of frameworks, structures and systems of global politics, global economies, global markets and global business philosophies, global societies and global value systems, global industries. This implies taking a directive and guidance role in global industry, economic, political development forums with the purpose of co-defining and co-emerging global future environments (e.g. World Bank, IMF, Portfolio committees of the UN, etc.). Knowledge work at this level manifests itself in the revealing of emergent level 7 global philosophies into meta-cognitive frameworks as basis for the emergence of global frameworks, structures, systems of global sustainability, be it political, economic, market, industry, social in nature. The debate around climate change with all its ramifications and implications for changes on a macro scale in all probability emerged from this context.

Context level 6 – Key characteristics:

- Co-determine or co-design the emergent global sustainable frameworks in the political, economic, market, industry, social spheres.
- Establish the nature of global principle, framework, and system design in the abovementioned domains that will advance global sustainability.

- Defining the **knowledge content** that will emerge credible global direction for systems of sustainability. The appropriateness or relevance of these emergent knowledge and systems content to global challenges will probably only become clear and possible to evaluate beyond 10 years.
- Based on fundamental understanding of global systems and frameworks, and more specifically those that may emerge as necessary for global sustainability, conceptualize, pre-empt and/or develop the global systems (political, economic, social, industry) necessary as pre-conditions for global sustainability.
- Establish global industry principles and frameworks that will enhance future global sustainability.
- Timeframe from initiation to evaluation beyond 10 years.

Context level 6 – Typical measurement areas/ measurement:

- Share price will inevitably reflect the leadership role in the industry globally.
- Global context and global industry sustainability.

Context level 6 – Typical kind of innovations:

- Complete reconfiguration of the political, economic, social, legal, industry principles, values and frameworks that will account for long-term global sustainability.

Value offering and principles for global futures (©Pieter Marais 2003) – Contextual Complexity level 7

This level transcends the emergent global frameworks of politics, economy, society and industry. It is about the emergence of a new value offering and principles for a new global future that may not have any clear and obvious relevance yet. Within the value offering and principles, the frameworks and inherent principles for the development of new future political, economic, social and industry dispensations are embedded. It is about the value offerings and philosophical principles that will benefit societies and industries still to come. Challenges at this level can be phrased in questions:

> What kind of value offerings or systemic frameworks, political, economic, social, industry, may the global environment need, beyond 20 years from now, to ensure global viability and sustainability?

> What principles, value framework and systems will appropriately support these global futures?

This is not a mere think-tank but an active process of conceptualizing and crafting global futures. Due to the long lead time attached to the emergence of the value at this level, people actively crafting these futures may never see the fruits of their endeavours. Here one can e.g. consider the work of Karl Marx which only came into its own after his death. It gave rise to the emergence of global socialism and was supported by a political, social and economic design of its own and even manifested in the Eastern block for a considerable period of time. Even now socialism is still a very active legacy.

IMPLICATIONS OF THIS CONTEXTUAL FRAMEWORK

It should be clear by now that Contextuality (a modified, enhanced, deeper appreciated SST) is a framework that describes the orders of contextual complexity and how this potentially manifests in work, people and organizations. It can also be seen as a meta-cognitive framework of complex systems and their contexts of which organizations and people are just two examples of complex systems. An in-depth understanding of the contextual framework, understanding or the lack thereof, clearly has critical implications on various fronts for organizations and people. An understanding results in a better appreciation of organizations and people in a more scientific way. This enhanced understanding, with potentially more appropriate action, includes the understanding of organization positioning, design, people contextual capability, careers and their development. It also assists in scientifically defining, designing, as well as contextualising other appropriate models to drive success.

This framework is not just another model that can be plugged into, or removed at will. It is clearly not just a dusting off of traditional grading systems. This framework is the meta-framework (the philosophy and basis for reference) that makes the difference between companies that effects integration and coherence versus those that constantly find themselves busy with "ad hoc-ism" (driving the latest and greatest short term fads) and confusion due to the lack of a framework that appropriately contextualises and integrates their approaches. It makes the difference between companies that "dumbify" their structures due to a lack of understanding or appreciating that people's contextual capability is what turns skills, knowledge and experience into appropriate value add. Without this understanding we continue to push people up the curve to where they become "incompetent" despite deep level skills and knowledge, unless we dumbify the organizational pitch and structure to reflect the actual contribution capability of people rather than the contextual value add from the organization into the market.

These and many other implications have called for two additional write-ups, which will follow soon. One will focus around the understanding and implications of this contextual framework in relation to organizations and the contexts of organization, the other in relation to people. It will deal with various issues, some of controversial nature. Below are some of the aspects that will be dealt with more comprehensively:

- Context and the "strategic pitch" of companies. An inappropriate pitch may result in value destruction and even demise of companies. An appropriate pitch may raise the organizational game plan.
  The pitch-appropriate design of companies based on "value-add". This will translate the strategic pitch of companies into a value add structural design (work, process and organization structure), the level specific design of organizational systems, determination of contextually appropriate accountabilities and measurements both at organizational as well as individual level, the design of a plethora of appropriately designed people related systems - remuneration, development, succession, performance management and others.

- It will contextualise scenario, strategic, business, production or service planning.
- It will clarify how design, structure and measurement of the organization and individuals within the organization focus and drive business activity and contribution towards the achievement of strategic objectives.
- It will assist in explaining why this framework is geared towards defining, measuring and managing value add and outputs rather than activities and inputs. It will also assist in explaining what accountability resorts where to enable maximum unlocking of this value add.
- On the converse side it will also explain current organizational designs and practices that contribute to value destruction in organizations. It will challenge the status hierarchies found in companies - a hierarchy where people achieve positions often through years of service rather than through quality of appropriate value add.
- It will explain the need for delayering of non-value adding multi-layered organizations and how to move towards a natural "hierarchy" of value add based on value adding context of roles and contributions.
- It will provide the key principles essential to enable a structure of **value-add** and **real contribution** to increase the likelihood of success in organizations.
- It will explain how the framework enhances organizational flexibility through the definition of role context. A process whereby a sense of continuity and consistency is established in an environment of continuous change. The nature (context) of contribution remains consistent even though the detail (content) may change. It will challenge the

appropriateness of systems and its implementation in support of business objectives. In this regard it will e.g. challenge the principles, design and practice of existing job grading systems, a large proportion of them inherently focussed on a vertical structure of importance, which increasingly are perceived as value inhibiting rather than value adding. Some efforts that have been made by certain entities to use SST as a grading framework need to be challenged. Old job grading principles have crept into the domain clouding the value generation qualities of the framework thereby effectively regurgitating the old rather than defining the new.

- It will help to define and describe the nature of contextual leadership and management qualities, capabilities and competencies necessary to achieve organizational objectives.

- It will challenge how remuneration and rewards in companies work today, especially in today's world of work that carries new and varied concepts of what is considered fair and equitable. A vertical pay structure no longer works in the "world of work" today. A fundamental redesign of reward systems is critical and should be disconnected from a job grading system as this connection results in the traditional trap of "skewing the structure to warrant the pay", thereby interfering with the clarity of role value generation.

- It will address the unnatural disparity in treatment between **managers and expert professionals** in organizations, which in many instances is a direct contributor to attrition of experts or professionals (leaders in their field). Experts are becoming highly mobile, joining other organizations, become expert consultants, or swelling the ranks of managers where they often become average or sometimes even ineffective managers. Managers and professionals can deal with similar levels of contextual complexity (the context). The difference can be found in the *content* of delivery.

Fairly often experts develop the essence, or vehicles, of value while the manager oversees the operationalisation and implementation thereof. Why should disparity then exist? Both managerial as well as professional functions can be found at all the levels of complexity. You may have engineers at lower as well as higher levels of complexity, human resource people at higher and lower levels of complexity, similar to managers at higher and lower levels of complexity. Currently, outdated systems, e.g. grading and pay systems, directly facilitate this disparity and thereby the destruction of value due to the loss of value generating professionals.

- It challenges the framework of development, career paths, progression and succession of people within organizations. Even today, in a much more horizontal and less vertical world, people still perceive vertical movement as the only movement in companies. That has an added complication in that expectations are created that any form of training or development should facilitate a vertical move. Contextuality provides for vertical as well as **horisontal** movement, training and development, progression, reward and more.

- It provides a context for fair, equitable and transparent recruitment practices.

- It facilitates ownership of work and contribution and also facilitates teamwork due to the potential of people being appropriately utilised, or at least given the opportunity to maximise their potential contribution and realise their capabilities. This, in turn, impacts on employee motivation.
- It also makes clear the management and leadership philosophy and practice whereby a culture of accountability is established as a result of employee accountability and control at source.

A number of organisational design, development, as well as Human Resources related technologies have already been developed to assist in dealing more appropriately with these challenges in context.

The above are just some of the impacts of the contextual framework within the organizational domain. When appropriately and effectively utilised, the framework impacts on everything a business does - its positioning, design, development, functioning, as well as its people, their recruitment, deployment, utilisation, development and more. Embarking on an understanding and utilisation of this framework is an exciting and never ending journey of learning that keeps on uncovering new dimensions and subtleties of the basic principles of the organizational "DNA" of CONTEXT and VALUE ADD.

References

1. Hoebeke Luc, Making Work Systems Better, John Wiley and Sons, Chichester, England, 1994.
2. Jaques & Cason, Human Capability, Cason Hall & Co, Fall Church, VA, 1994.
3. Jaques E, Requisite Organization, Cason Hall & Co, Revised 2nd Edition, Arlington, VA, 1996.
4. Marais P, Various internal research & development write-ups and internally published documents/articles 1995 – 2009.
5. Stamp G, Various Internally published articles, Brunel Institute for Organization and Social Studies, Auxbridge, UK.

www.ingramcontent.com/pod-product-compliance
Lightning Source LLC
Chambersburg PA
CBHW071229170526
45165CB00003B/1051